AF375217

Senior Days

Poetry by Alice L. Mohor

Illustrations by Carol J. Mohor

Senior Days

Poetry by Alice L. Mohor

Illustrations by Carol J. Mohor

ISBN 979-8-9900028-4-5

Published by

Bilbo Books Publishing
www.BilboBooks.com
bilbobookspublishing@gmail.com
(706)-549-1597
Athens, Georgia

Printed in the United States of America

table of contents

then

boomer child............ 7

childhood 9

special 11

station wagon..........13

toys 15

push-pedal cars.......17

backyard playset......19

triumph................... 21

challenge 23

racing 25

kick-the-can 27

down the shore....... 29

another way 31

ocean waves 33

end of summer........ 35

novelties 37

new 39

magazines............... 41

scout camp.............. 43

going on a
bear hunt 45

driftwood................ 47

skating.................... 49

flexible flyer............51

slides 53

now

companions.............. 55

displaced 57

entangled 59

justified 61

progress.................. 63

technology 65

connected 67

discharge 69

handsfree 71

attention.................. 73

SUV 75

courage................... 77

clarity...................... 79

closed captioning...... 81

mystery 83

complicated 85

older....................... 87

catching up 89

um........................... 91

extreme.................. 93

check-up 95

hygiene................... 97

boomerang.............. 99

balance 101

humbled..................103

autumn years.........105

persist 107

joint
replacement...........109

physical therapy 111

short term
memory..................113

tests......................115

friends...................117

back cover

relativity

alm . 6

boomer child

my soldier dad
who had been brave
returned from war
in a great wave

he went to school
married his wife
anxious to start
a normal life

with children in
a happy home
for memories
in kodachrome

far better than
the youth he knew
when all the world
was thrown askew

alm . 8

childhood

palisades park
we could not go
the wave pool might
spread polio

a march of dimes
on movie screens
then needle sticks
with piercing screams

sugar cubes in
the high school gym
to save us from
booster shots grim

but chicken pox
measles and mumps
kept us at home
with itchy bumps

alm . 10

special

on saturdays
more time to eat
bisquick pancakes
with syrup sweet

grilled sandwiches
hot melted cheese
tomato soup
a lunch to please

ice cream between
two waffles hot
a delight that
would hit the spot

just once a year
my turn to take
a corner piece
of birthday cake

station wagon

a new rambler
for family fun
with room enough
for everyone

automatic
shift transmission
two tone fins a
space age vision

for lounging a
wide chaise format
the front seatback
reclined to flat

hamburgers or
milkshakes to go
for a drive-in
giant screen show

LINC

toys

from lincoln logs
to tinker toys
the best fun things
were made for boys

blocks for building
peg boards with holes
rockets to launch
with switch controls

erector sets
electric trains
girls did not need
to use their brains

handwork or jacks
baby doll stuff
hopscotch or ropes
not near enough

alm • 16

push-pedal cars

bright and shiny
the model new
two little cars
the color blue

cruising along
the sidewalk wide
we had great fun
ride after ride

with one behind
we pedaled fast
around the block
our world was vast

lap after lap
day after day
driving our cars
in happy play

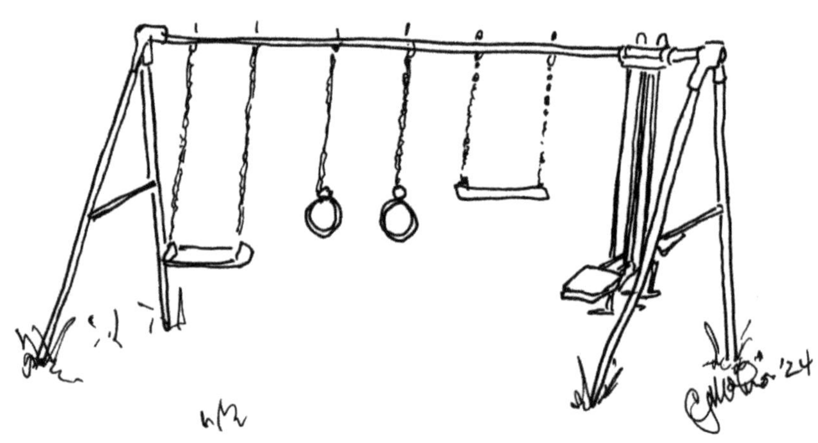

backyard playset

our hand-me-down
had swings to pump
to rise and fall
or stall and jump

one neighbor had
swings and a slide
and double seats
to share a ride

another had
a slide and swings
and trapeze bar
with set of rings

that i could reach
and hold with ease
to dare and hang
by just my knees

triumph

a bicycle
at cost far less
from cousins sent
by rail express

heavy and blue
with black tires wide
the seat too tall
to stand astride

afraid to fall
my learning slow
i worried i
might never know

the joy i felt
when i did ride
and the freedom
it did provide

alm . 22

challenge

to balance on
a pogo stick
was early on
a daunting trick

but after time
i could rebound
to jump along
on level ground

and later bounce
uphill and back
without a land
on sidewalk crack

to then declare
myself the best
a champion
above the rest

go, go, go!
No, No, Nooo...

racing

my blue cruiser
different from
what sleek new bikes
had then become

an older frame
with fat tires wide
made for a smooth
but heavy ride

i did not like
to speed downhill
a turn too fast
might make me spill

but i could pump
without a stop
to catch them up
before the top

2, 3, 4 . . . 10. . .60, HERE I COME

kick the can

in summertime
with supper done
at eventide
we would have fun

outside before
the sun would set
until the dark
would drag a net

with neighbor kids
we all would play
a friendly game
to end the day

of hide and seek
and flee and chase
to kick a can
away from base

down the shore

the ocean waves
high tide or low
stormy or calm
always a show

water to swim
with beach to walk
white sand for play
or rest or talk

lone and tandem
we kids would ride
on heavy bikes
with fat tires wide

canasta games
or solitaire
a simple time
with little care

another way

i could not seem
to get the knack
of floating still
upon my back

or turn to take
a breath in quick
with a crawl stroke
or flutter kick

until the day
dad said to me
keep your head up
then you can see

to swim along
upon the tide
while your arms pull
and legs kick wide

alm . 32

ocean waves

when little a
small ripple wave
was big enough
for me to brave

it took some time
to go beyond
the shallow depth
of tidal pond

out deeper than
the trough of shells
to swim and dive
and float the swells

to where the surf
would curl and break
to catch a ride
before the wake

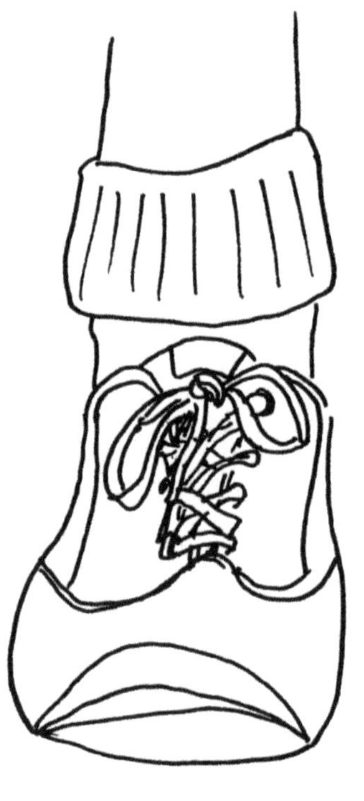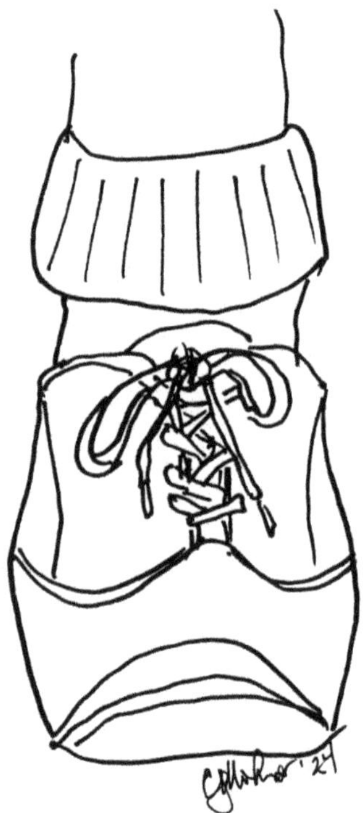

end of summer

once every year
i remember
first days of school
in september

new shoes to wear
with good support
and leather soles
not meant for sport

a jacket light
or cardigan
to wear or just
bring home again

my room to find
with friends to greet
and sometimes new
classmates to meet

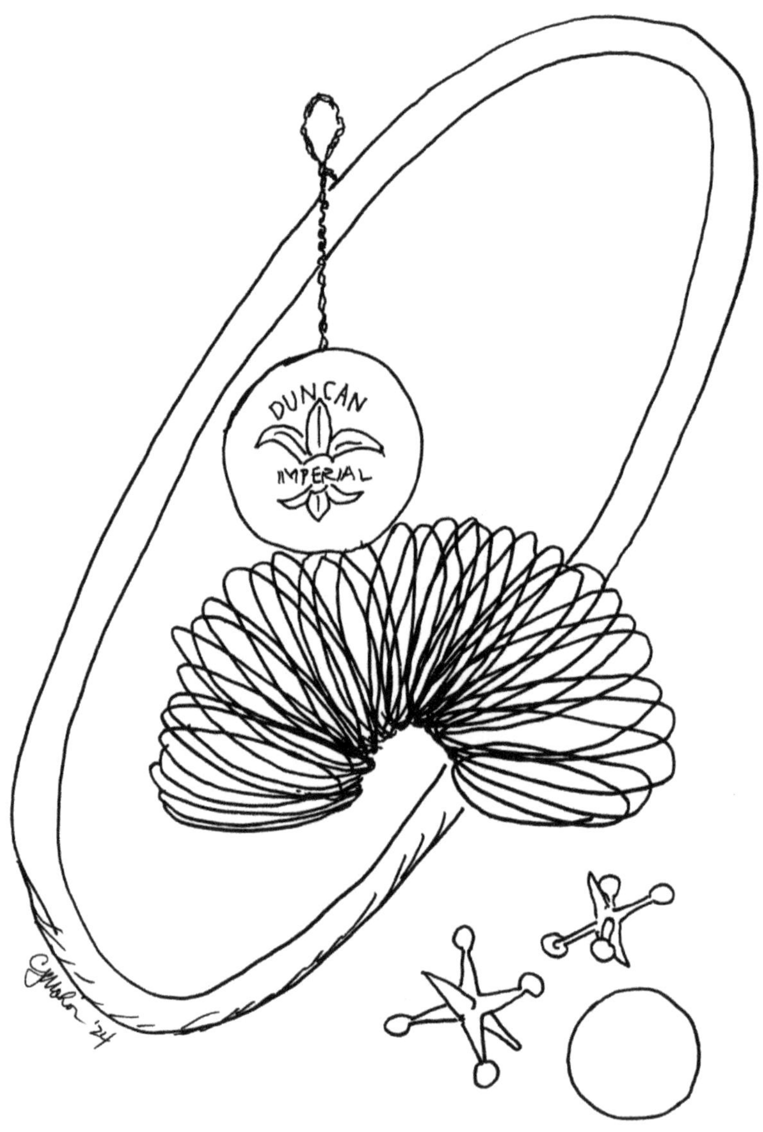

DUNCAN
IMPERIAL

novelties

a slinky toy
to walk the stair
without a stop
from here to there

sleeping yo-yos
that would obey
returning when
cast out away

silly putty
to stretch or tear
or bounce up high
into the air

a hula hoop
to make gyrate
with body parts
that undulate

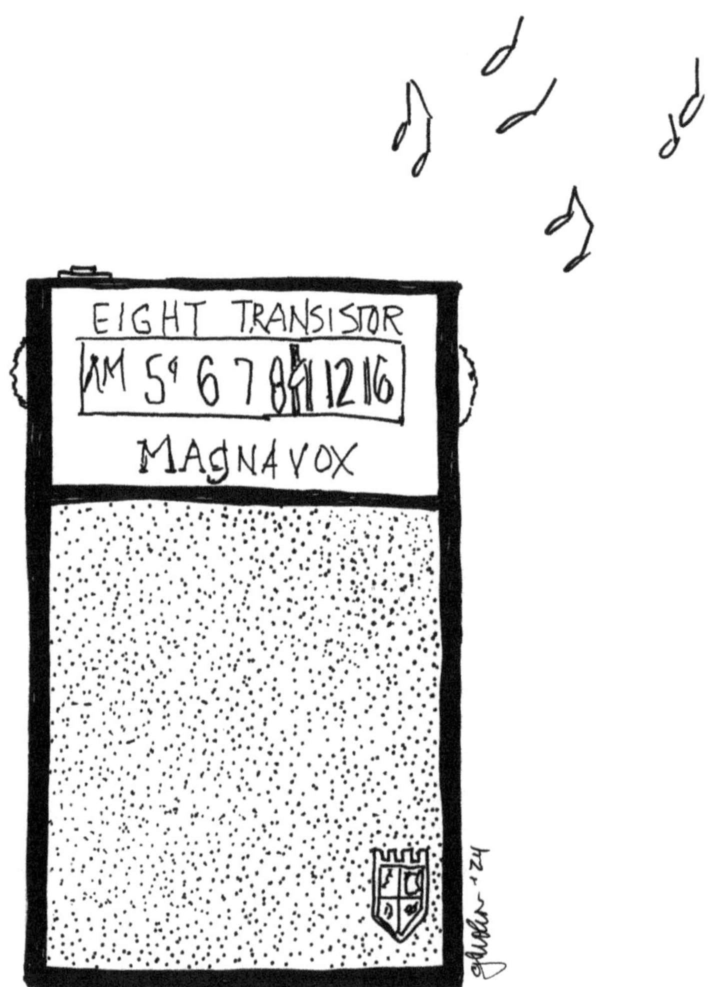

EIGHT TRANSISTOR
AM 5 6 7 8 11 12 16
MAGNAVOX

new

a transistor
small radio
to take along
where we would go

outside to walk
or ride a bike
when in the car
or on a hike

onto the beach
or at a pool
or waiting for
the start of school

to hear the game
or a new hit
from a pocket
where it would fit

LOOK
THE GENERAL MARSHALL PAPERS
LIFE
PRINCESS TO QUEEN ELIZABETH

magazines

something active
my leisure need
i did not like
to pleasure read

not one to choose
a chapter book
but magazines
like Life or Look

captions under
the photographs
were just enough
to hold my grasp

for a story
in voices told
by images
direct and bold

alm . 42

scout camp

pine branch railing
a sleeping loft
metal bunkbeds
mattresses soft

an outside pump
to push and pull
then walk uphill
with milk can full

wood burning stove
fireplace of stone
no TV set
no telephone

unlike our home
modern and new
we found old things
to play and do

alm . 44

going on a
bear hunt

when 8 years old
a brownie scout
but long before
a tent camp out

we gathered in
an open field
obedient
we all did yield

to form a great
big circle wide
and did as told
by adult guide

in echoing
words and actions
one of many
fun distractions

driftwood

winter weekends
spent down the shore
included one
specific chore

to supplement
the propane heat
that barely warmed
a few square feet

we combed the beach
high water line
for wood worn smooth
by rolling brine

to restock our
shrinking supply
fireplace fuel
we need not buy

skating

in wintertime
on cold days nice
we sometimes got
to skate on ice

motion of a
different sort
unlike the type
of schoolyard sport

gliding atop
thin blades of steel
our bodies had
a special feel

sensation once
beyond compare
when outside in
the crisp clear air

flexible flyer

sledding on snow
a winter thrill
sliding all day
down a tall hill

a running start
then belly flop
careening to
a sudden stop

or riding down
a backyard run
time and again
till day was done

then inside for
a tasty treat
to warm us with
hot cocoa sweet

1960
12
1974
36
1965
22

slides

thirty-six full
carousel trays
enough to view
for days and days

convention trips
vacation fun
playing outside
in summer sun

homecoming floats
circle line cruise
banquet dinners
picturesque views

holidays and
graduations
and birthdays all
celebrations

companions

excited dogs
bark while i yawn
up out of bed
just after dawn

to start and stop
a walk uphill
pausing to smell
then mark at will

stretching out from
left side to right
our wide parade
a trying sight

as drivers rush
to race with time
our early walk
a lazy climb

alm . 56

displaced

upon the floor
to stretch and bend
as someone lithe
did recommend

i faithfully
strain to adhere
with effort spent
to persevere

in contorted
replications
of maneuvered
demonstrations

all while the dogs
that i displace
wait patiently
to claim their space

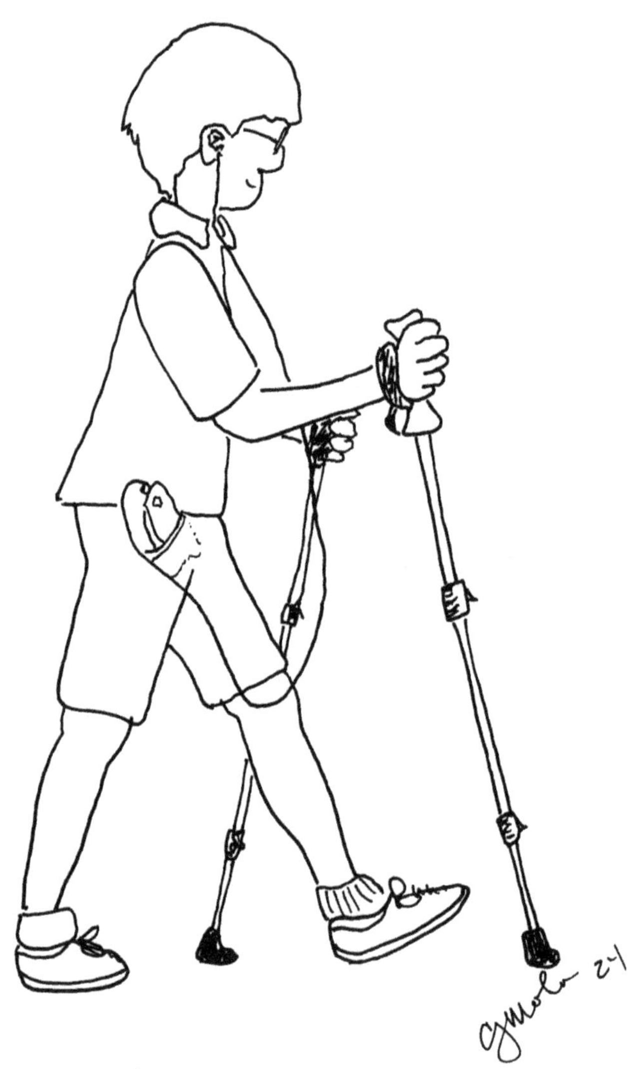

entangled

thirty minutes
five days a week
my walk involves
a new technique

walking with poles
my wrists in straps
i stride and swing
around in laps

a circle path
with level pitch
streaming until
a podcast glitch

when i must stop
to extricate
while my step count
declines in rate

justified

i do accept
and recognize
the healthy part
of exercise

that keeps me fit
to enjoy more
all that my life
may have in store

but day to day
what i like best
is the joy of
the guilt-free rest

that i spend in
more lazy fun
because i got
my work-out done

NEW
MODEL

progress

i take the time
to search and ask
for the right thing
to do a task

or for a fit
that feels just right
looks good but not
too loose or tight

then wear or use
with quiet glee
made perfectly
as if for me

but when i seek
to buy one more
the new one is
not as before

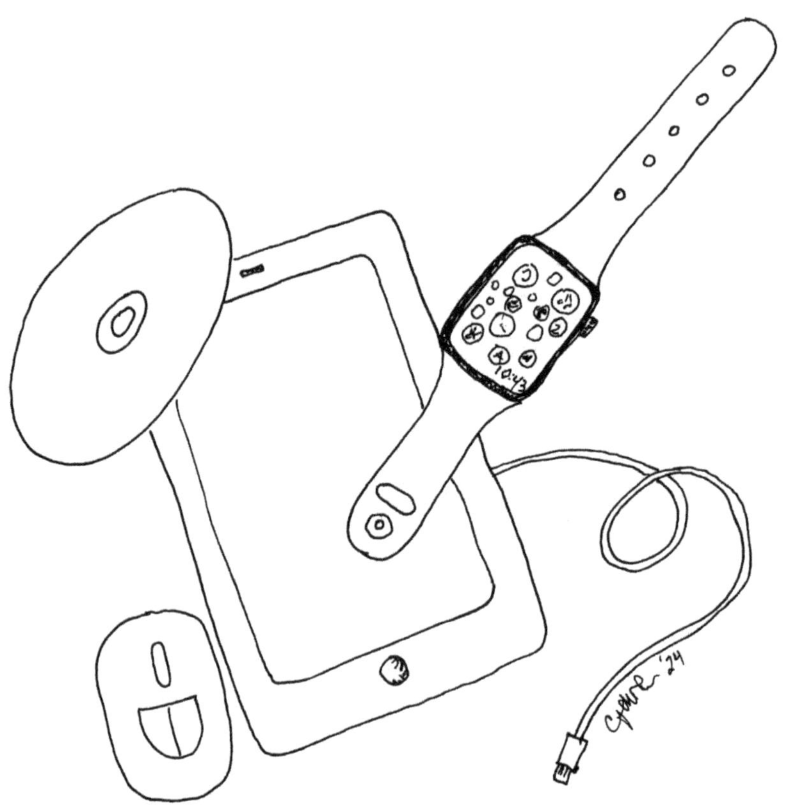

alm . 64

technology

technology
can frustrate me
i grew up with
typewriter key

magnetic tape
computer disc
external drive
advancement brisk

ethereal
cloud data file
zoom meeting calls
now standard style

in awe of those
who step in time
the pace of change
almost a crime

connected

bound albums were
for photographs
music was played
on phonographs

movies were viewed
in theater seats
or living rooms
as old repeats

cellular phones
do more than call
pocket wonders
now do it all

with watches worn
around the wrist
to guarantee
nothing is missed

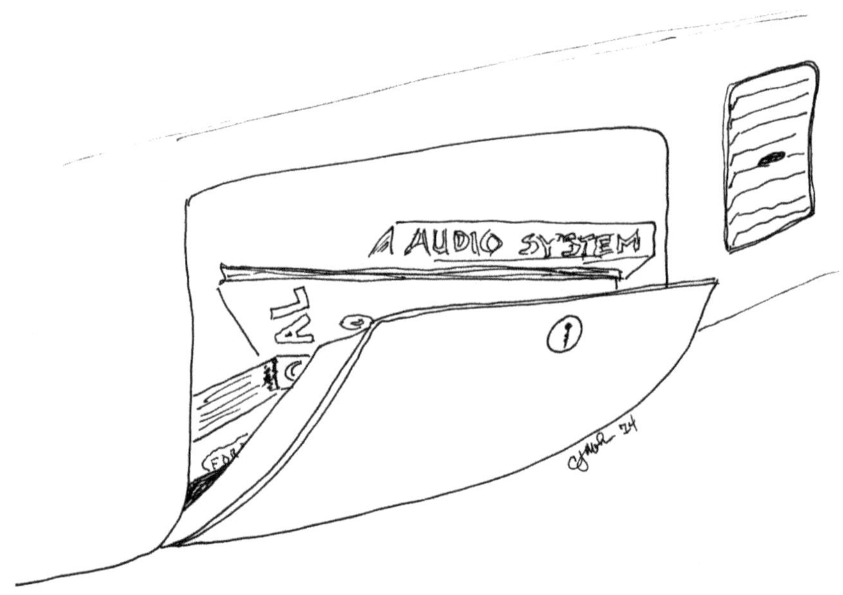
A AUDIO SYSTEM
AL

discharge

movies music
and even more
my car now has
features galore

every option
so very new
requires more
than quick review

3 manuals
with pages thick
need study more
than skimming quick

smart features are
more challenge than
learning to play
just like chopin

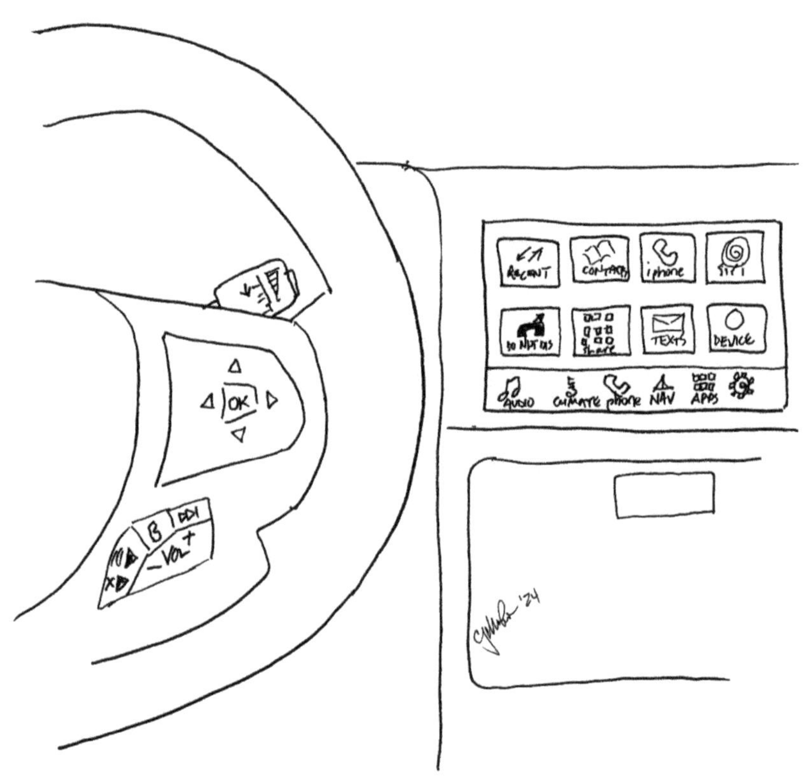

OK
VOL+
B
RECENT
CONTACTS
iphone
SIRI
DO NOT DISTURB
TEXTS
DEVICE
AUDIO
CLIMATE
PHONE
NAV
APPS

handsfree

my accent not
of neutral sound
but speech like mine
does wide abound

understood by
those around me
chatting with friends
always carefree

but for the times
my cell phone sync
frustrates me near
beyond the brink

when once again
i must entreat
by shouting from
my driver's seat

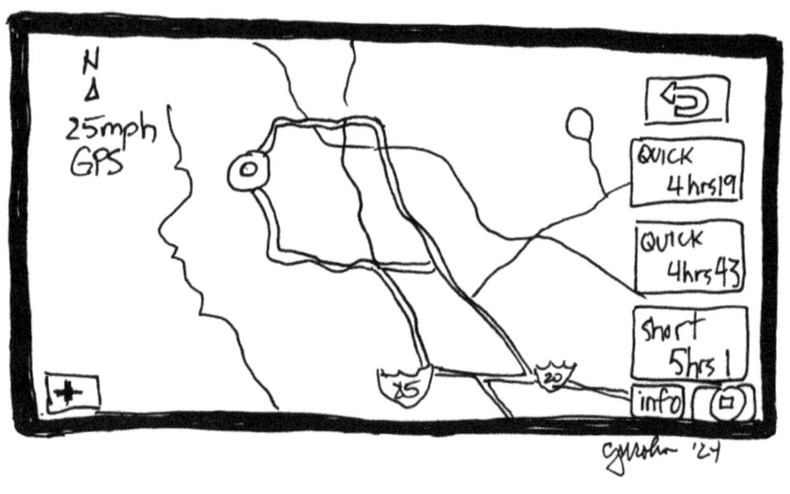

N
25mph
GPS
QUICK
4hrs19
QUICK
4hrs43
short
5hrs1
info
25
20

attention

the routine of
familiar turns
allows me to
relax concerns

with confidence
i will set out
i know the way
without a doubt

navigating
by GPS
can elevate
my driving stress

though dutifully
i do comply
my efforts take
me right on by

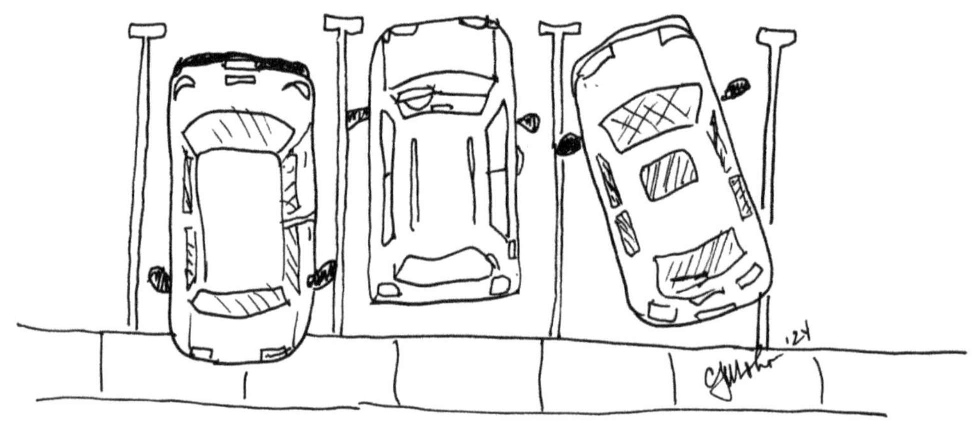

alm . 74

SUV

routine for me
now redefined
to park my car
and be aligned

a challenge that
is daunting though
a mastered skill
met long ago

in a heavy
vehicle large
responsive as
an ocean barge

that i could slip
precise and quick
in one great arc
practiced and slick

STOP
KJL 295

courage

once a highway
enthusiast
multiple lanes
cars passing fast

maneuvering
with easy skill
routine without
alarm or thrill

moving into
another lane
easily done
no stress or strain

but a left turn
across a lane
is now for me
a constant bane

DELFI
TONIGHT
GONE WITH THE WIND

clarity

broadcast series
in black and white
would mesmerize
my mind each night

or movies from
the classic age
when perfect stars
were all the rage

stories told by
innuendo
scored to end in
full crescendo

that i now see
through adult eyes
in wonderment
of former guise

CC on
Hey, I said one or two lumps of sugar?
SAMSUNG

closed captioning

sound systems now
are super great
but people please
enunciate

gone are the days
of slow clear speech
when far back rows
a voice could reach

in eloquent
perfect technique
as actors once
would broadly speak

but method now
the only way
and i must read
all that they say

mystery

serialized
with drama fraught
i wait to see
who will be caught

but sometimes i
too soon forget
a character
from the outset

whose name i do
not recognize
the next week in
quick plot reprise

deprived of a
full scene review
i have to watch
without a clue

alm . 84

complicated

dramatic with
characters fraught
bad TV guys
were always caught

but story lines
now weave and turn
or make the truth
hard to discern

now i must watch
with attention
to enable
comprehension

as tension builds
to quickened height
which later will
strange dreams ignite

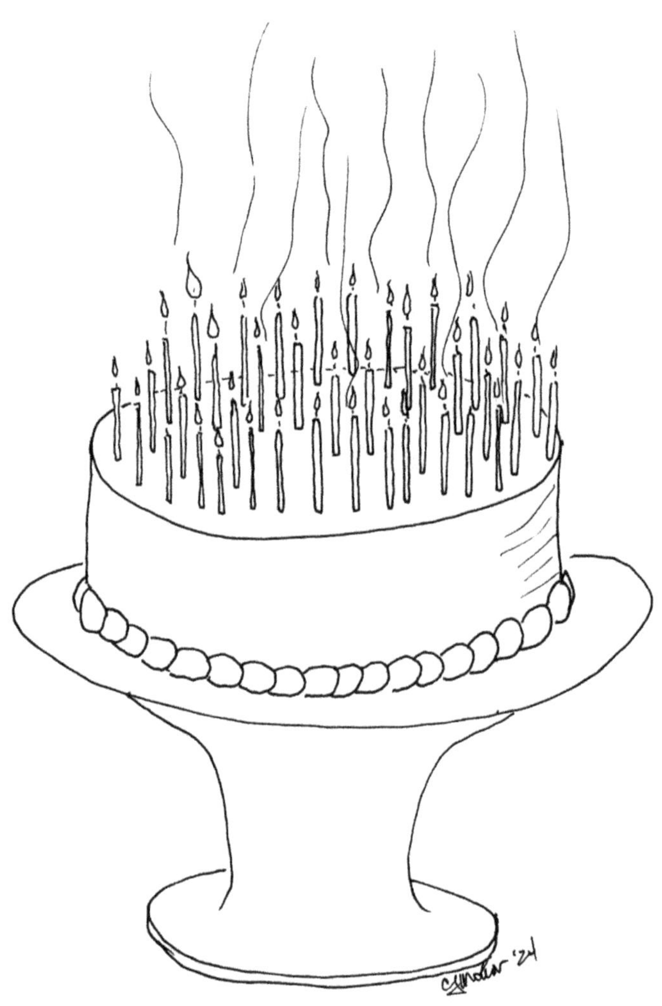

alm . 86

older

happily we
would look toward
birthdays moving
ever forward

expectations
have altered since
aging is marred
by movement's wince

after milestones
to mark ahead
we consider
things yet to dread

and celebrate
our faculties
despite loose skin
and creaky knees

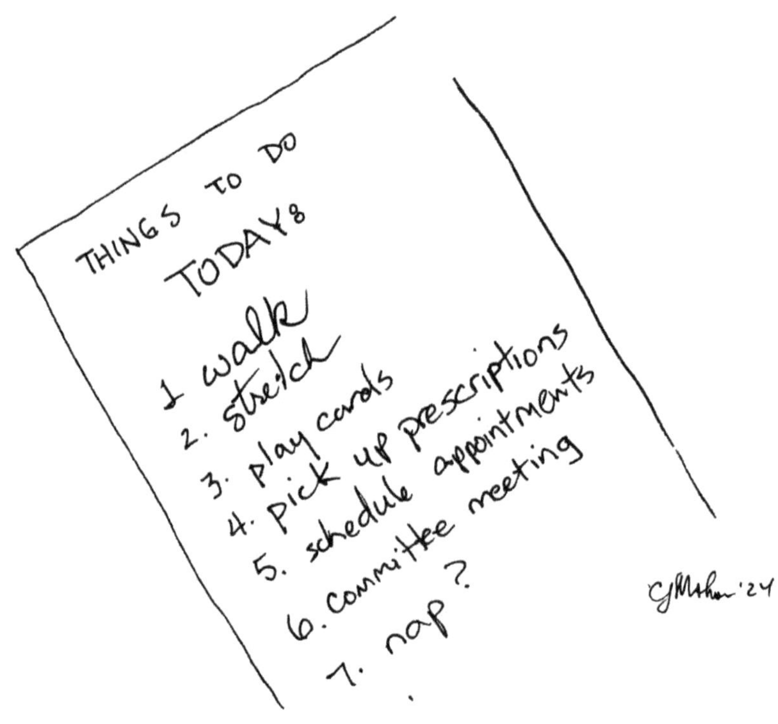

THINGS TO DO
TODAY:
1 walk
2. stretch
3. play cards
4. pick up prescriptions
5. schedule appointments
6. committee meeting
7. nap?

catching up

once we would chat
of dating fun
attentions sought
or sadly done

once we would shout
events of joy
wedding then birth
of girl or boy

once we would boast
of job reward
with accolades
to look toward

but now we share
as soldiers do
the challenges
we must push through

alm . 90

um...

more frequently
what first frustrates
and finally
exasperates

is the word lost
that would convey
exactly what
i want to say

or action i
plan next to do
that disappears
without a clue

of what i just
had on my mind
but cannot the
next second find

POLAR
BEAR
PLUNGE

extreme

our synapses
might better fire
if we embrace
a practice dire

a dip or swim
in routine bold
by jumping in
to water cold

and stimulate
connections new
inhibiting
brain plaque like goo

that would impair
connection link
to twist the brain
and make it kink

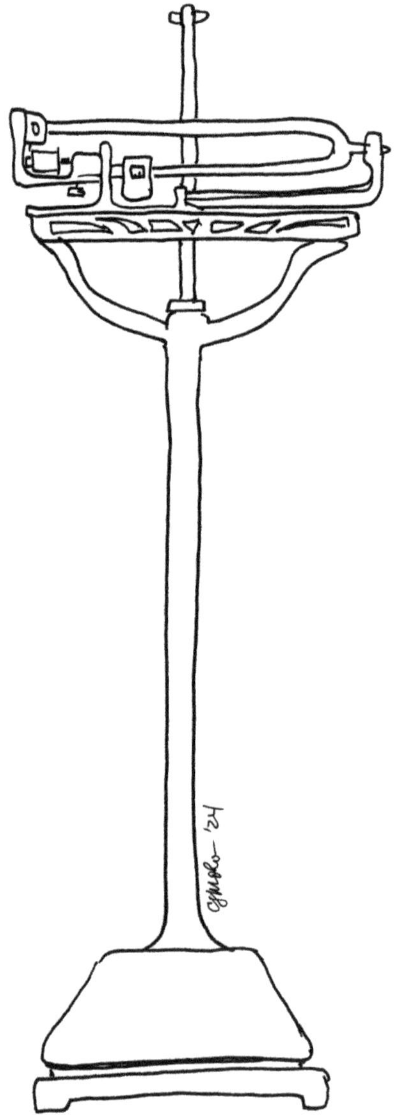

alm . 94

check-up

when i was young
few were taller
my classmates were
mostly smaller

i now admit
to losing height
as i strain to
stand more upright

before a look
of some disdain
with lecture to
at last refrain

from eating as
i could before
lest present girth
increases more

alm . 96

hygiene

to ready for
a night of sleep
a regiment
i now must keep

in order to
prevent decay
recession or
wearing away

before i brush
i waterpik
then floss or thread
no part done quick

too wide awake
i lie and stare
lamenting all
this dental care

boomerang

my fourth grade year
spring vacation
was one of great
consternation

i spent that week
plus one week more
with chicken pox
i did abhor

no playing out
in fresh air sun
after the cold
of winter done

oh how unfair
in later life
for shingles to
again cause strife

balance

when a toddler
my diapered seat
cushioned my fall
from misplaced feet

a stumble when
i played outside
seldom did more
than break my stride

or might produce
a bruise or scrape
set right with just
some gauze and tape

now injuries
occur at will
when tripping or
when standing still

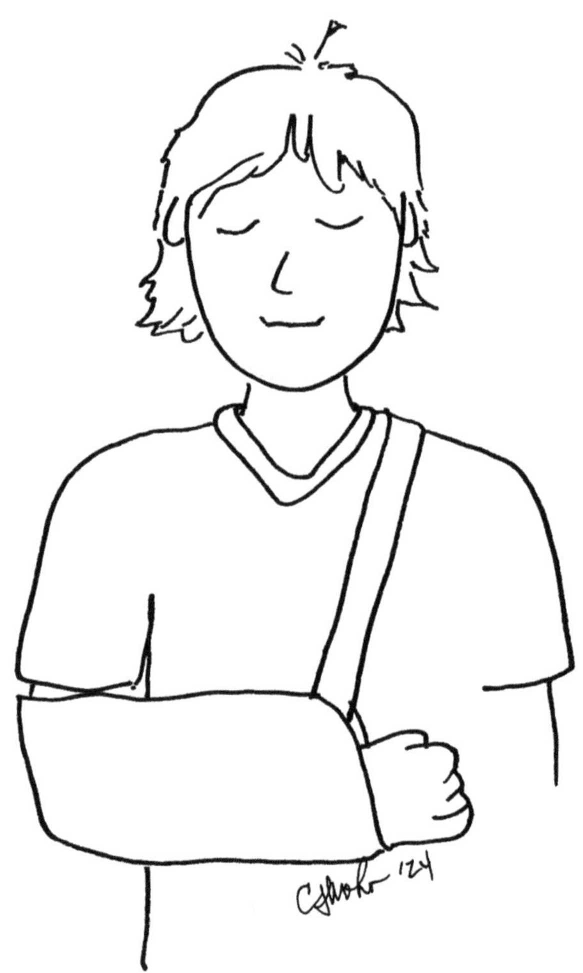

humbled

tilting beyond
what feet could right
my agile grace
no longer light

but then to find
beyond my pride
an injury
i cannot hide

a bruise that will
take days to fade
or cut or scrape
to then parade

or damage that
will need repair
for broken bone
or tissue tear

autumn years

the skeletons
of halloween
may dance a line
of serpentine

but my bone ends
are not as free
my joints are worn
at hip and knee

my supple youth
of strength and range
has over time
succumbed to change

an afternoon
of heavy use
will next day feel
much like abuse

alm • 106

persist

i wake up with
my thumb stuck bent
a problem new
to now lament

humbled again
by past abuse
small maladies
seem more profuse

especially
since now with age
no certainty
time will assuage

what once would heal
with only rest
might now mandate
a lengthy quest

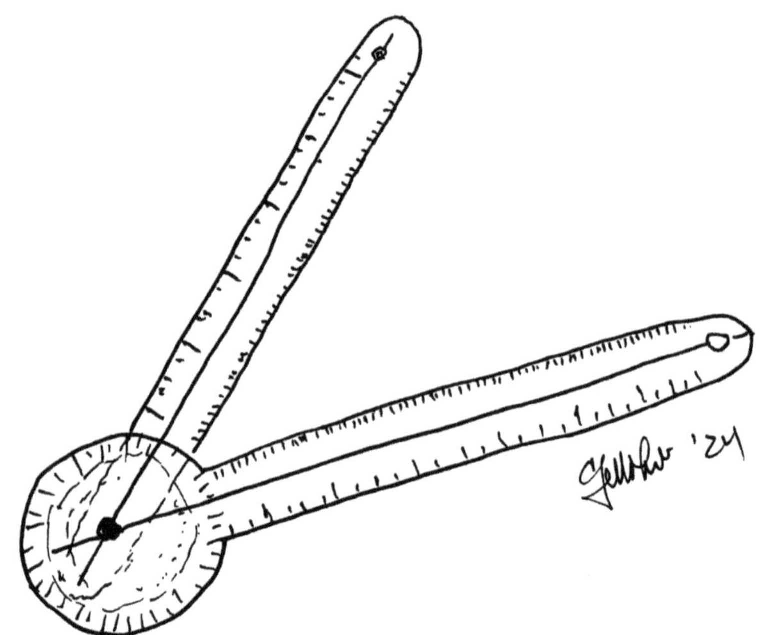

joint replacement

when joints worn out
by fits and starts
need maintenance
with replaced parts

movement ease will
take time to earn
with exercise
you work to learn

for motion won
by small degree
for your new hip
shoulder or knee

part stainless steel
wow lucky you
now super strong
and rust free too!

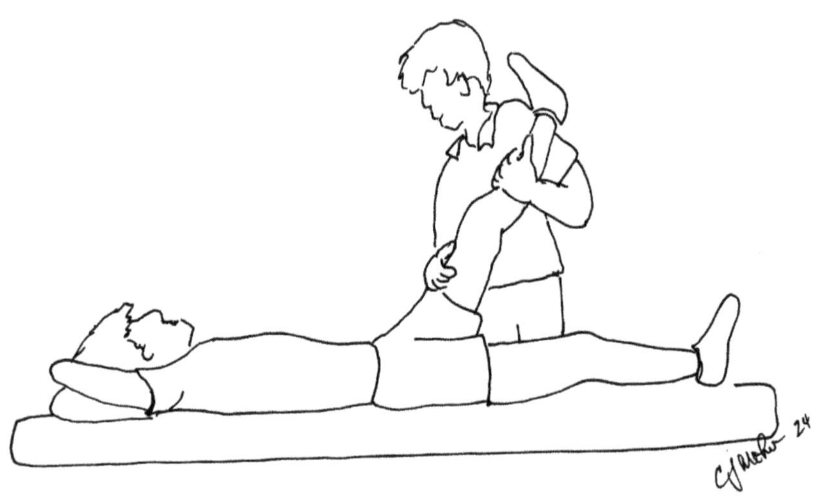

physical therapy

a warm-up first
to tenderize
before a round
of exercise

done with a count
in group of 10
to please repeat
time and again

with stretches for
motion increase
short of extreme
rupture release

then followed by
a rest with cold
positioned in
a wrestle hold

FEBRUARY
SUNDAY
what a day! Wrote apron to church
herself to doctors who else good. Called
brother and had a great . . . .
MONDAY

short term
memory

my journal has
4 lines of space
to write in and
yesterday trace

recalling tasks
that i had done
some notable
some just for fun

encounters planned
or unforeseen
that lift me from
my sole routine

to acknowledge
and celebrate
that every day
can become great

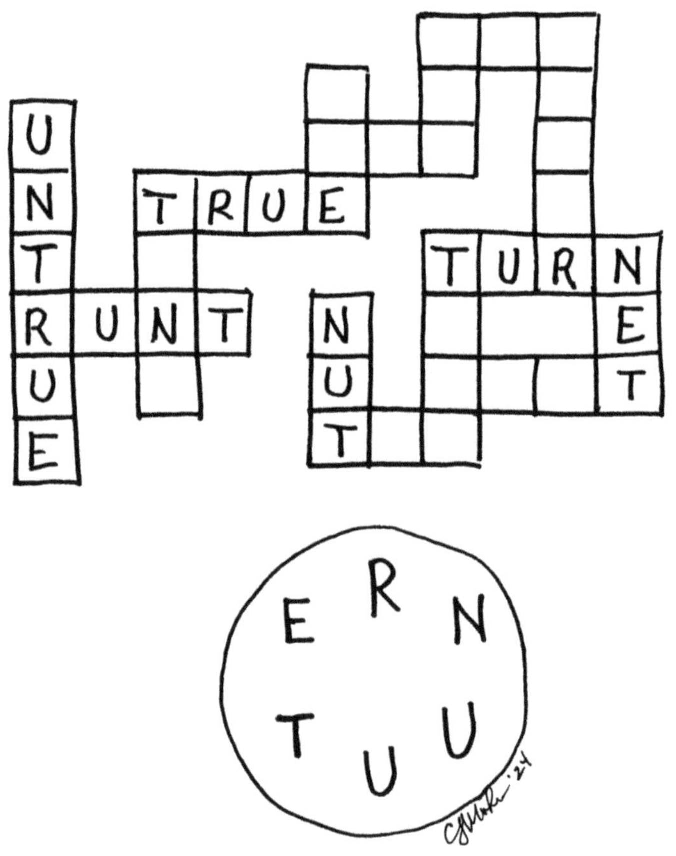

tests

before finals
a reading day
meant for study
but not for play

memorizing
concepts and facts
while ignoring
all that distracts

out the window
or down the hall
till late at night
or birdsong call

now daily games
to puzzle lest
my brain retreats
to early rest

friends

we walk with poles
we stand up slow
we mostly drive
to where we know

we mind the speed
we take our time
we read and write
and even rhyme

we still persist
despite our fear
with each advance
of elder year

we know we are
by each day blessed
our oldest friends
remain our best

Alice Louise Mohor began writing rhyming poetry for her elementary physical education students, and continues to write for children and adults in retirement.

Carol Jean Mohor began illustrating her sister's rhyming poetry while teaching elementary art, and continued to illustrate her sister's poetry into retirement. This book is Carol's fourth collaboration with Alice.